CLASSIC TRUTHS

for

TRIUMPHANT LIVING

Great Themes from Romans

BIBLE STUDY GUIDE

From the Bible-teaching ministry of

Charles R. Swindoll

INSIGHT FOR LIVING

Chuck graduated in 1963 from Dallas Theological Seminary, where he now serves as the school's fourth president, helping to prepare a new generation of men and women for the ministry. Chuck has served in pastorates in three states: Massachusetts, Texas, and California, including almost twenty-three years at the First Evangelical Free Church in Fullerton, California. His sermon messages have been aired over radio since 1979 as the *Insight for Living* broadcast. A best-selling author, Chuck has written numerous books and booklets on many subjects.

Based on the outlines and transcripts of Chuck's sermons, the study guide text is co-authored by Bryce Klabunde, a graduate of Biola University and Dallas Theological Seminary. He also wrote the Living Insights sections.

Editor in Chief:
Cynthia Swindoll

Coauthor of Text:
Bryce Klabunde

Assistant Editor:
Wendy Peterson

Copy Editor:
Deborah Gibbs

Text Designer:
Gary Lett

Graphic System Administrator:
Bob Haskins

Director, Communications Division:
Deedee Snyder

Creative Services Manager:
John Norton

Project Coordinator:
Colette Muse

Printer:
Sinclair Printing Company

Unless otherwise identified, all Scripture references are from the New American Standard Bible, © The Lockman Foundation 1960, 1962, 1963, 1968, 1971, 1972, 1973, 1975, 1977. Used by permission. The other translations cited are the *King James Version* [KJV] and *The Living Bible* [LB].

CONTENTS

1   The Classic Gospel   1
      Romans 1:1, 7–17

2   The Classic Problem   8
      Romans 1:18–32

3   The Classic Remedy* 17
      Romans 4:1–8; Ephesians 2:1–9

4   The Classic Battle 25
      Romans 6:1–14; 7:7–21

5   The Classic Victory 33
      Romans 8:1–17, 31–39

6   The Classic Sacrifice 41
      Romans 12:1–3

    Books for Probing Further 51

    Ordering Information/Order Forms 53

*This message was not part of the original series but is compatible with it.

INTRODUCTION

The dictionary defines *classic* as "a work of enduring excellence." The key word here is *enduring*—a rare quality in our day.

We live in a world of paper cups, throwaway cartons, and disposable contact lenses. Nothing is meant to last anymore, not even our relationships or values. No wonder so many have lost their sense of stability and inner peace.

Much as our culture fights it, though, we human beings *need* that which endures. We need to anchor our drifting selves to something that lasts, something of excellence, something that's held true throughout the generations. That is precisely what we'll find in Paul's letter to the Romans.

Romans is Paul's *magnum opus*, a true classic that delves into such themes as our helpless, sinful state . . . God's gracious, saving gospel . . . our struggle against sin . . . our victory through God's all-powerful Spirit.

These truths are exciting—and definitely life-changing. So journey along with me as we visit several scenic sites on Paul's Roman road to triumphant living, and make your life a classic!

Chuck Swindoll

PUTTING TRUTH
INTO ACTION

K nowledge apart from application falls short of God's desire for His children. He wants us to apply what we learn so that we will change and grow. This study guide was prepared with these goals in mind. As you go through the following pages, we hope your desire to discover biblical truth will grow as your understanding of God's Word increases and that you will be encouraged to apply what you've learned.

To assist you in your study, we've included a section called Living Insights at the end of each lesson. These exercises will challenge you to study further and to think of specific ways to put your discoveries into action.

There are many ways to use this guide—in personal devotions, group studies, discussions with friends and family, and Sunday school classes. And, of course, it's an ideal study aid when you're listening to its corresponding *Insight for Living* radio series.

To benefit most from this study guide, we would encourage you to consider it a spiritual journal. That's why we've included space in the Living Insights for recording your thoughts and discoveries. We hope you'll return to those sections often for review and encouragement as you continue to grow in your walk with Christ.

Bryce Klabunde

Bryce Klabunde
Coauthor of Text
Author of Living Insights

CLASSIC TRUTHS

for
TRIUMPHANT LIVING

Great Themes from Romans

Chapter 1

THE CLASSIC GOSPEL
Romans 1:1, 7–17

Luther called the book of Romans "the true masterpiece of the New Testament."[1] Coleridge applauded it as "the profoundest piece of writing in existence."[2] The early church fathers christened it "the cathedral of the Christian faith."[3] What makes Romans such a towering book? Author Eugene Peterson explains.

> The letter to the Romans is a piece of exuberant and passionate thinking. This is the glorious life of the mind enlisted in the service of God. Paul takes the well-witnessed and devoutly believed fact of the life, death, and resurrection of Jesus of Nazareth and thinks through its implications. How does it happen that in the death and resurrection of Jesus, world history took a new direction, and at the same moment the life of every man, woman, and child on the planet was eternally affected? What is God up to? What does it *mean* that Jesus "saves"? What's behind all this, and where is it going?
>
> These are the questions that drive Paul's thinking. Paul's mind is supple and capacious. He takes logic and argument, poetry and imagination, Scripture and prayer, creation and history and experience,

1. Martin Luther, as quoted by Donald Grey Barnhouse in *Man's Ruin: Romans 1:1–32* (Grand Rapids, Mich.: William B. Eerdmans Publishing Co., 1952), vol. 1, p. 2.

2. Samuel Taylor Coleridge, as quoted by J. Sidlow Baxter in *Explore the Book* (Grand Rapids, Mich.: Zondervan Publishing House, Academie Books, 1960), p. 66.

3. Attributed to Chrysostom.

and weaves them into this letter that has become
the premier document of Christian theology.[4]

This "premier document," the *magnum opus* of all Paul's writings,
champions the premier message of Christianity: the gospel of Jesus
Christ. As we'll see in this portion of Paul's letter, God's good news
(the meaning of *gospel*) "is the power of God for salvation," His
very righteousness revealed (Rom. 1:16, 17).

When we explore the gospel, then, we enter holy ground. We
encounter God's saving presence, His strong and compassionate
nature. So before setting out on this study, you may want to spend
a few moments in prayer. Take some time to prepare your heart and
mind, asking God, as the psalmist did, "Lead me in Thy truth and
teach me, For Thou art the God of my salvation; For Thee I wait
all the day" (Ps. 25:5).

A Little Orientation

In studying any book of the Bible, we'll find several basic facts
helpful for understanding its message.

The Identity of the Writer

The correspondence of Paul's day, unlike our letters today, always began by telling who wrote the letter:[5]

> Paul, a bond-servant of Christ Jesus, called as an
> apostle, set apart for the gospel of God. (Rom. 1:1)

In addition to his name, Paul offers two credentials. First, he is
"a bond-servant of Christ Jesus," emphasizing his voluntary and
total commitment to Christ. According to commentator Donald
Barnhouse, the laws of Moses required that slave owners liberate
their slaves after seven years of service. However, if the masters
were kind, the servants could choose to remain as slaves for the
rest of their lives. They would be taken to the doorpost of the
tabernacle where a priest would pierce their ear with an awl, per-
manently marking them as "bondslaves."[6] That is how Paul sees

---

4. Eugene H. Peterson, *The Message: The New Testament in Contemporary English* (Colorado
Springs, Colo.: NavPress, 1993), introduction to Romans.

5. Paul's *amanuensis*, or secretary, Tertius did the actual penning of this letter from Paul's
dictation (see Rom. 16:22).

6. Barnhouse, *Man's Ruin*, pp. 8–9.

himself in relation to Christ. Because of Christ's overwhelming kindness toward him, Paul was His slave by choice for life.

His second credential is that he has been "called as an apostle." This statement sets forth his authority as Christ's emissary. Christ Himself had called Paul on the road to Damascus, transforming him from a self-appointed persecutor of Christians to a God-appointed proclaimer of the gospel (see Acts 9:1–16; Gal. 1:1, 11–24). He was "set apart" for a completely new life work—to announce, exposit, and defend God's message of salvation.

The Identity of the Recipients

Paul addresses his thoughts to

all who are beloved of God in Rome, called as saints. (v. 7a)

His readers, like himself, were set apart by God—taken from the dominion of darkness and reoriented to the kingdom of light (see Acts 26:18). That's all *saints* means—being given the position of holy children in God's family.

That doesn't mean we are perfect or that we live set apart in a perfect world. Rather, we are now lights in this darkened world, same as the Roman saints were. They too lived in

an age when things seemed, as it were, out of control. Virgil wrote: "Right and wrong are confounded; so many wars the world over, so many forms of wrong. . . ."

It was a world where violence had run amok. When Tacitus came to write the history of this period, he wrote: "I am entering upon the history of a period, rich in disasters, gloomy with wars, rent with seditions, savage in its very hours of peace." . . . It was an age of moral suicide.[7]

Into the turmoil and ugliness of this scene Paul bestows "grace to you and peace from God our Father and the Lord Jesus Christ" (Rom. 1:7b). If God's kindness and purity were needed anywhere, they were needed here.

---

7. William Barclay, *The Letter to the Romans*, rev. ed., The Daily Study Bible Series (Philadelphia, Pa.: Westminster Press, 1975), pp. 30–31.

The Reasons for Writing

Paul's reasons for writing this letter were both personal and theological. Notice his warm tone in the following verses:

> First, I thank my God through Jesus Christ for you all, because your faith is being proclaimed throughout the whole world. For God, whom I serve in my spirit in the preaching of the gospel of His Son, is my witness as to how unceasingly I make mention of you, always in my prayers making request, if perhaps now at last by the will of God I may succeed in coming to you. For I long to see you in order that I may impart some spiritual gift to you, that you may be established. (vv. 8–11)

Paul desired to affirm and encourage their faith (v. 8) and to assure the Roman believers of his care, evidenced by his constant prayers (vv. 9–10a). He also wanted them to know how much he longed to see them (vv. 10b–11a). And he yearned to pass on truth and build into their faith (v. 11b).

Slowly and steadily, Paul climbs to the overarching theological reason he had writing his letter: to clarify the gospel of grace, particularly to his beloved Gentiles.

A Classic Presentation

Paul's treatise on Christ's gospel begins with three noteworthy "I am" statements.

> I am under obligation both to Greeks and to barbarians, both to the wise and to the foolish. (v. 14, emphasis added)

"I feel this driving passion, this calling," Paul confesses, "to reach all people with God's message."

> Thus, for my part, I am eager to preach the gospel to you also who are in Rome. (v. 15, emphasis added)

Paul is so excited about God's mercy and grace, he can shout the Good News of redemption from the rooftops!

> For I am not ashamed of the gospel, for it is the power of God for salvation to everyone who believes,

to the Jew first and also to the Greek. (v. 16, emphasis added)

Paul can be proud of the gospel because it is backed up by the sure power of God. The word *power, dunamis* in Greek, has been linked to the image of dynamite. Everett Harrison, however, counters that view.

> This is quite out of place, for the emphasis is not on blowing false religions out of the way or blasting a trail of success for the true faith or even on delivering people from habits they have been unable to shake off. . . . The stress falls not on [power's] mode of operation but on its intrinsic efficacy. It offers something not to be found anywhere else—a righteousness from God.[8]

This power, though silent, internal, and unseen, transforms the lives of "everyone who believes" (v. 16).

And note: Paul did not add anything after the word *believes* in verse 16. Salvation comes through belief in the Lord Jesus Christ— plus nothing. This is what the Scriptures call *justification*, which we can define as "the supernatural, sovereign act of God whereby He declares righteous believing sinners while they are still in a sinning state" (see Rom. 5:6–9). Even though we have sinned and deserve all the punishment sin should bring, we have been *declared* righteous—not *made* righteous[9]—while still in a sinning state.

What makes this possible? Our righteous, sincere works? Our diligent human effort? Won't these outweigh our sinfulness? No, our earnest attempts at righteousness will always fall short because they cannot escape the taint of sin. Only God's righteousness, only our reliance on His mercy and grace through Christ, can bring about salvation.

> For in [the gospel] the righteousness of God is revealed from faith to faith; as it is written, "But the righteous man shall live by faith." (1:17; see also Eph. 2:1–9)

---

8. Everett F. Harrison, "Romans," *The Expositor's Bible Commmentary*, gen. ed. Frank E. Gaebelein (Grand Rapids, Mich.: Zondervan Publishing House, Regency Reference Library, 1976), vol. 10, pp. 18–19.

9. To be made righteous implies moral perfection—a state we won't achieve until we reach heaven. It's a true statement that Christians aren't perfect, just forgiven.

In the face of a humanity that's helplessly sinful, no wonder Paul was eager to shout about a God who is so unreasonably gracious as to impart His own righteousness to us!

An Application of the Gospel

Truth this crucial cannot be admired and then carefully shelved under a glass case. It needs to be dealt with. It requires a response. And that doesn't mean simply studying it or learning all the nuances of it; it demands belief. As the hymnwriter said,

> My hope is built on nothing less
> Than Jesus' blood and righteousness;
> I dare not trust the sweetest frame,
> But wholly lean on Jesus' name.
>
> On Christ, the solid Rock, I stand:
> All other ground is sinking sand.[10]

The gospel is a narrow message, not in keeping with our society's emphasis on inclusiveness at all costs. But it's the truth and the only way we can be saved (see Acts 4:10–12).

Our response to the gospel of Jesus Christ, then, determines our destiny. If we refuse Christ's offer of salvation, we turn away from life and choose death—both now and forever. But if we believe God and accept the gift of His grace, then we are destined for eternal life.

This Good News is the message of Romans, the foundation of the literary cathedral that Paul built almost two thousand years ago. It is the classic gospel, and it will never lose its power to transform a person's life. Has it transformed yours?

 Living Insights

We build our hope for a secure future like carpenters build a house. First, we frame the structure with a good education. Then we carefully attach the wood siding of a promising career. To keep us warm, we insulate ourselves with a loving family. And to protect us during financial storms, we build a roof made of savings accounts

---

10. Edward Mote, "The Solid Rock," in *The Hymnal for Worship and Celebration* (Waco, Tex.: Word Music, 1986), no. 402.

and insurance policies.

After all the boards are in place, we will finally live safe and secure. Or so we think.

Layoffs can splinter our promising career. Conflicts can destroy our loving family relationships. Unexpected expenses can strip the tiles off our savings accounts. Or calamity can strike. Perhaps the doctor says we have a life-threatening illness, and death, the leveler of all hope, starts whipping through the eaves.

At times like these, even the strongest walls split and crumble. Whether we cave in or remain standing depends on one thing— our foundation.

Look back at the hymn we quoted earlier, "The Solid Rock." We sing these words in church, but do we understand them? What do you think it means to build your hope "on nothing less Than Jesus' blood and righteousness"?

_____

_____

The gospel is "the power of God for salvation to everyone who believes" (Rom. 1:16). From the following verses, what are some of the ways the gospel exercises God's power for you?

John 1:12 _____

Romans 8:10–11 _____

Colossians 1:13 _____

Colossians 2:13–14 _____

1 John 5:11–12 _____

Has your house of hope been shaken lately? Have you been trusting that your beams and rafters will hold firm while forgetting to rest in your foundation? The hymnwriter proclaims, "I dare not trust the sweetest frame, But wholly lean on Jesus' name." Take a moment to express to the Lord your faith in Him for your salvation. Only He is our solid Rock—"All other ground is sinking sand."

_____

_____

_____

Chapter 2

THE CLASSIC PROBLEM
Romans 1:18–32

What is the classic problem of the world? Poverty? Racism? War? These are heart-wrenching dilemmas to be sure, but they're just the symptoms of underlying illness. Charles H. Spurgeon, the eloquent preacher of the nineteenth century, cuts down to the diseased core of the human condition:

> Sin is the mother and nurse of all evil, the egg of all mischief, the fountain of bitterness, the root of misery. Here you have the distilled essence of hell, the quintessence, as the old theologians would say, of everything that is unlovely, disreputable, dishonest, impure, abominable—in a word—damnable.[1]

Sin. From this cancerous cell, all of humanity's ills have multiplied. We tend to blame social problems, like ignorance and poverty for our misbehaviors, but the true disease lies within us. We are sinners by birth, living in the shadow of death, hiding from the wrath of God.

God's Wrath

Focusing on sin and doom is a difficult task. No one enjoys learning that he or she has a malignancy. Yet which is worse—for a doctor to conceal the truth and let the patient die, or reveal the awful facts so the patient can pursue a cure?

In the last half of Romans 1, Paul assumes the role of a physician, handing the world a chilling diagnosis. It's one that's guaranteed to wipe the smile off the face of the most optimistic person. It cuts deep into our hearts, yet its pain can bring life if we listen closely and heed the doctor's somber warning.

The Fact

For the wrath of God is revealed from heaven

---

1. Charles H. Spurgeon, *Spurgeon at His Best,* comp. Tom Carter (Grand Rapids, Mich.: Baker Book House, 1988), pp. 191–92.

against all ungodliness and unrighteousness of men, who suppress the truth in unrighteousness. (v. 18)

According to commentator Donald Grey Barnhouse, Paul had a choice of two Greek words for *wrath*:

> one of them meaning the hot, vehement surge of anger, and the other the slowly rising indignation. The first word, *thumos*, which signifies a panting rage from a root that means "to breathe violently," is not used here; but the word, *orga*, which signifies an indignation that has risen gradually and become more settled. Its original meaning was connected with plants and fruits in their swelling with juice until they finally burst.[2]

When writing verse 18, Paul chose *orga*, the gradual indignation, which reflects the Lord's longsuffering nature in dealing with us. He's not a spiteful, temperamental Zeus, who throws lightning bolts at anyone who steps out of line. His wrath is a judicious reaction to evil—a holy aversion that, for now, is restrained behind the great dam of His patience. One day, it will burst forth in a flood of judgment. Meanwhile, it is continually revealed throughout history, as people from every culture and time have had to drink the bitter consequences of their sin.

The objects of His wrath are not people but "ungodliness and unrighteousness"—two trunks out of which all branches of wickedness grow. *Ungodliness* is the sin against God's being, sprouting such evils as idolatry and unbelief. It is living as if there is no God, and it leads to *unrighteousness*—the sin against God's will. From this sin grow the weedy tendrils of immorality, enmity, and rebellion.

The Reason

Why is it necessary for God to reveal His wrath? Because humankind gives Him no choice. We have suppressed the truth and rejected the evidence He has emblazoned across creation.

> Because that which is known about God is evident within them; for God made it evident to them. For

---

2. Donald Grey Barnhouse, *Man's Ruin: Romans 1:1–32* (Grand Rapids, Mich.: William B. Eerdmans Publishing Co., 1952), vol. 1, p. 219.

since the creation of the world His invisible attributes, His eternal power and divine nature, have been clearly seen, being understood through what has been made. (vv. 19–20a)

According to the psalmist, nature shouts God's presence:

> The heavens are telling of the glory of God;
> And their expanse is declaring the work of His
> hands. (Ps. 19:1)

The evidence for God's existence is everywhere. It echoes through the great canyons, crashes in waves on the seashore, and shoots like the stars in the night sky. It even whispers to us within our own hearts. Yet we plug our ears, refusing to listen to a higher authority than ourselves. As a result, Paul says, we "are without excuse" (Rom. 1:20b). No one can claim ignorance to justify sin.

Humanity's Sin

In spite of all the arrows of nature pointing to God, people have stubbornly chosen to follow their own path. In verses 21–32, Paul diagnoses three general ways we express this defiant spirit: idolatry, immorality, and iniquity.

Idolatry

Throughout history, people have worshiped idols instead of God. Their descent into idolatry followed a definite pattern. First, they willfully *ignored* God.

> For even though they knew God, they did not honor
> Him as God, or give thanks. (Rom. 1:21a)

Second, they cleverly *imitated* God. They didn't just neglect Him, they arrogantly crowned themselves king and made their judgments and opinions, rather than God's laws, the rule of their lives. As a result,

> they became futile in their speculations, and their
> foolish heart was darkened. Professing to be wise,
> they became fools. (vv. 21b–22)

Ultimately, they totally *replaced* God. Paul says that they

> exchanged the glory of the incorruptible God for an

10

image in the form of corruptible man and of birds and
four-footed animals and crawling creatures. (v. 23)

Humankind was created to worship the Creator. Without God,
though, people turned to worship creation. First they bowed to
images of themselves, then to images of animals. The downward
spiral didn't end until they were groveling before idols of snakes
and lizards. What a pitiful scene!

Sadly, like the heartbroken father of the Prodigal Son, God let
people go the way of their own choosing.

> Therefore God gave them over in the lusts of
> their hearts to impurity, that their bodies might be
> dishonored among them. For they exchanged the
> truth of God for a lie, and worshiped and served the
> creature rather than the Creator, who is blessed for-
> ever. Amen. (vv. 24–25)

No fate could be worse than God abandoning us to ourselves.
Three times in this passage, Paul tolls the death knell: "God gave
them over . . . gave them over . . . gave them over" (see also
vv. 26, 28). William Barclay explains the devastating implications
for the sinner:

> It is not that God is punishing him; he is bringing
> punishment upon himself and steadily making him-
> self the slave of sin. The Jews knew this, and they
> had certain great sayings upon this idea. "Every ful-
> fillment of duty is rewarded by another; and every
> transgression is punished by another." . . .
>
> The most terrible thing about sin is just this
> power to beget sin. It is the awful responsibility of
> free will that it can be used in such a way that in
> the end it is obliterated and a man becomes the
> slave of sin, self-abandoned to the wrong way. And
> sin is always a lie, because the sinner thinks that it
> will make him happy, whereas in the end it ruins
> life, both for himself and for others, in this world
> and in the world to come.[3]

---

3. William Barclay, *The Letter to the Romans*, rev. ed., The Daily Study Bible Series (Philadelphia, Pa.: Westminster Press, 1975), pp. 29–30.

Immorality

From idolatry, the next step down is immorality. Because when God gives us over to our own passions, we don't get better; we get worse. Society's problems don't straighten out; they get more tangled. We don't evolve to higher levels of love and virtue; we sink to the depths of our basest natures.

> For this reason God gave them over to degrading passions; for their women exchanged the natural function for that which is unnatural, and in the same way also the men abandoned the natural function of the woman and burned in their desire toward one another, men with men committing indecent acts and receiving in their own persons the due penalty of their error. (vv. 26–27)

Homosexuality, like any sexual sin, is the culmination of three "exchanges" that people make on their way to self-destruction. First, they exchange the glory of God for an image of man, elevating themselves as their only spiritual authority (v. 23). Second, they exchange the truth of God for a lie, redefining what's right and wrong (v. 25). Cut loose from God and His truth, they are free to drift with lust's tide wherever it may lead. Homosexuality represents the final destination for some and the ultimate exchange—the natural for the unnatural, the pure for the perverted.[4]

Iniquity

Haven't we arrived at the bottom of depravity's pit? No, not yet. In verses 28–32, Paul's scalpel slices away the fetid bandages of human denial, revealing the fully inflamed wickedness of the depraved mind:

> And just as they did not see fit to acknowledge God any longer, God gave them over to a depraved mind, to do those things which are not proper, being filled with all unrighteousness, wickedness, greed, evil; full of envy, murder, strife, deceit, malice; they

---

4. Many people claim that homosexuality is simply a "sexual preference" or an "alternate lifestyle." But Paul clearly states that homosexuality is more than just different; it is "unnatural," "degrading," "indecent," and an "error." For people caught up in this struggle, there is hope in Christ. But, like anyone in sin, they must first face the hard truth about their behavior.

are gossips, slanderers, haters of God, insolent, arro-
gant, boastful, inventors of evil, disobedient to par-
ents, without understanding, untrustworthy, unloving,
unmerciful; and, although they know the ordinance
of God, that those who practice such things are
worthy of death, they not only do the same, but also
give hearty approval to those who practice them.

In this list, Paul gathers people from all levels of society. Gang
members line up beside corporate raiders; prostitutes, beside church
gossips; skinheads, beside Ph.Ds. The same heinous evil that fired
the ovens in the Nazi concentration camps burns in our hearts as
well. We dare not point fingers of judgment at anyone. Only because
of Christ's redeeming power and the Spirit are we able to oppose
the darkness inside of us and align ourselves with His light.

Three Responses

The disfigured and diseased face behind humanity's mask horrifies us. What can we do? We have three choices, each of which
will shape the direction of our entire lives.

Our first choice is *passivity*. In his book *World Aflame*, Billy
Graham described the danger of this attitude:

Mr. Average Man is comfortable in his complacency
and as unconcerned as a silverfish ensconced in a
carton of discarded magazines on world affairs. . . .
Modern man has become a spectator of world
events, observing on his television screen without
becoming involved. He watches the ominous events
of our times pass before his eyes, while he sips his
beer in a comfortable chair. He does not seem to
realize what is happening to him. He does not understand that his world is on fire and that he is about
to be burned with it.[5]

As Christ's salt and light, we need to be part of the answer—not
part of the tolerant majority, sighing an "Oh, well" in front of the TV.

Another response is *anxiety*. We let our fear of a sinful world
commandeer our common sense. We triple-bolt our doors and bar

5. Billy Graham, *World Aflame*, Crusade edition (Minneapolis, Minn.: Billy Graham Evan-
gelistic Association; New York, N.Y.: Doubleday and Company, 1965), p. 15.

our windows. We start carrying handguns, just in case. Categorizing people as either "us" or "them," we build tall, barbed-wire fences to keep the "bad people" away. Certainly, this was not the attitude of Christ.

The best response is *availability*. This perspective says, "Lord, I realize that, except for Your grace, I would be struggling in a pit of sin so deep that I'd never climb out. I am available as a minister of the gospel, to speak whenever, in whatever circumstances, and in whatever way that would honor You to people who have lost their hope."

Which response will you choose?

 Living Insights

"The truth about man is terrifying," writes Charles Colson and Ellen Santilli Vaughn in their book *The Body: Being Light in Darkness*. They illustrate their point with a gripping story.

> In 1960, Israeli undercover agents orchestrated the daring kidnapping of one of the worst of the Holocaust masterminds, Adolf Eichmann. After capturing him in his South American hideout, they transported him to Israel to stand trial.
>
> There, prosecutors called a string of former concentration camp prisoners as witnesses. One was a small haggard man named Yehiel Dinur, who had miraculously escaped death in Auschwitz.
>
> On his day to testify, Dinur entered the courtroom and stared at the man in the bulletproof glass booth—the man who had murdered Dinur's friends, personally executed a number of Jews, and presided over the slaughter of millions more. As the eyes of the two men met—victim and murderous tyrant— the courtroom fell silent, filled with the tension of the confrontation. But no one was prepared for what happened next.
>
> Yehiel Dinur began to shout and sob, collapsing to the floor.
>
> Was he overcome by hatred . . . by the horrifying memories . . . by the evil incarnate in Eichmann's face?

No. As he later explained in a riveting "60 Minutes" interview, it was because Eichmann was not the demonic personification of evil Dinur had expected. Rather, he was an ordinary man, just like anyone else. And in that one instant, Dinur came to the stunning realization that sin and evil are the human condition. "I was afraid about myself," Dinur said. "I saw that I am capable to do this . . . exactly like he."

Dinur's remarkable statements caused Mike Wallace to turn to the camera and ask the audience the most painful of all questions: "How was it possible . . . for a man to act as Eichmann acted? . . . Was he a monster? A madman? Or was he perhaps something even more terrifying . . . was he normal?"

Yehiel Dinur's shocking conclusion? "Eichmann is in all of us."[6]

We'd like to draw a line between us and truly wicked people— the Charles Mansons, the Ted Bundys, the Adolf Eichmanns of the world. We're not depraved like they are . . . are we?

The same beast that drove them to commit horrible atrocities lives within all of us. Each of us is capable of the worst sorts of evil.

Have you been feeding the beast within you, perhaps secretly indulging it, letting it loose here or there? If so, in what ways?

Perhaps you think you can tame your sin nature. A little bit of sin, and no more. "I'm in control. I can stop whenever I want." Have you been telling yourself that? What has been the outcome?

---

6. Charles Colson with Ellen Santilli Vaughn, *The Body: Being Light in Darkness* (Dallas, Tex.: Word Publishing, 1992), pp. 187–88.

Sin is too powerful for you or anyone to tame. It will turn on you before you realize what's happened. By then, however, it's too late. Only Jesus Christ has beaten the beast. Take a moment to admit your need for Christ. Surrender to Him your vain attempts to handle sin.

_____

_____

_____

_____

_____

Has this been a dark and disturbing chapter for you? In the next chapter, we'll skip ahead to Romans 4, where Paul reveals the remedy for the problem of sin. So get ready, the sun is about to dawn!

Chapter 3

THE CLASSIC REMEDY

Romans 4:1–8; Ephesians 2:1–9

"Anything worth having is worth working for." "Nobody gets something for nothing." "Hard work never hurt anybody."

These are the slogans of a society built on the foundation of a strong work ethic. Since childhood, we are taught to knuckle down and work for everything we get; and the more valuable the thing we want, the harder we will have to work.

If you want a car, work for it . . . a luxury car, work harder. If you want a house, work for it . . . a grander house, work harder. If you want to retire, work for it . . . to retire in style, work harder . . . HARDER . . . *HARDER!*

The problem is, many of us don't know when to quit. We get hooked on the perks, power, and prestige of our jobs. We begin to measure our worth by how many hours we're logging and the number of responsibilities we have. Before we realize it, we've stopped working to live and started living to work. Our career has become our idol.

Immersed in a culture that worships work, we're likely to approach salvation with that same mind-set. After all, if we work to get something good and work harder to get something really good, something eternal must cost a lifetime of labor, right?

Nothing could be further from the truth.

The Grace-Faith Transaction according to Romans

Our work ethic has become one of the most formidable enemies of grace. In his commentary on Romans, Donald Grey Barnhouse wrote,

> man is incurably addicted to doing something for his own salvation, and, therefore, it is most difficult for him to accept the doctrine of pure grace.[1]

Has your earn-what-you-need mentality weighed you down and hindered you from enjoying the freedom of the gospel? The apostle

---

This message was not a part of the original series but is compatible with it.

1. Donald Grey Barnhouse, *God's Remedy* (Grand Rapids, Mich.: William B. Eerdmans Publishing Co., 1954), vol. 3, p. 293.

17

Paul declares some good news that is certain to lift the heavy burden from your shoulders.

Declaration

The theme of Paul's epistle of grace is crystallized in one verse:

> For we maintain that a man is justified by faith apart
> from works of the Law. (Rom. 3:28)

The Living Bible is even more direct:

> We are saved by faith in Christ and not by the good
> things we do.

This verse means that salvation is free—which, in our no-free-lunch culture, immediately raises suspicion. "OK," we squint, "where's the fine print?"

There is no fine print. We couldn't earn our salvation even if God commanded us to. Why? Because we "are all under sin" (v. 9). Paul explains the extent of our problem in verses 10–18:

> As it is written,
>   "There is none righteous, not even one;
>   There is none who understands,
>   There is none who seeks for God;
>   All have turned aside, together they have
>   become useless;
>   There is none who does good,
>   There is not even one."
>   "Their throat is an open grave,
>   With their tongues they keep deceiving,"
>   "The poison of asps is under their lips";
>   "Whose mouth is full of cursing and bitterness";
>   "Their feet are swift to shed blood,
>   Destruction and misery are in their paths,
>   And the path of peace have they not known."
>   "There is no fear of God before their eyes."

We are totally depraved. That doesn't mean we're worthless worms, nor does it mean we've committed every conceivable atrocity. Rather, it means that corruption permeates us through and through. We are not as bad as we can be; we are as *bad off* as we can be. Sin soils even our cleanest garments, so that all of us "fall short of the glory of God" (v. 23).

Picture a transient rummaging through a trash bin, then stepping into a sterile operating room to perform surgery. It's unthinkable! He's grossly unclean, grossly unskilled, grossly inadequate. Yet that's what it would be like for us to step into heaven in our sin-stained condition. What we need is a cleansing . . . a transformation . . . a miracle.

Paul unveils that miracle in verse 24:

> Being justified as a gift by His grace through the redemption which is in Christ Jesus.

We sometimes use the word *justify* to mean proving someone is innocent. That's not how Paul uses the word. We are guilty; there's no disputing that fact. Rather, by justifying us, He *pronounces* us innocent, clean, and pure. He declares us righteous while we are still in a state of sin.[2]

God offers this decree to us "as a gift by His grace." Justification is a "grace-gift"—it's free. No one can buy or earn it, but that doesn't mean it comes without cost.

Paul's phrase "the redemption which is in Jesus Christ" draws our eyes to the staggering price tag of our salvation. *Redemption* means to release someone by paying a ransom. A kidnapper may demand millions of dollars for the release of a loved one; but to free us from Satan's claim, Jesus had to pay the ultimate price—His own life.

On the cross, Jesus paid our ransom with His blood. As a result, no more work remains for us. "It is finished!" Jesus cried (John 19:30). All we must do is humbly and gratefully receive His gift of eternal life.

Illustration

This teaching must have stunned the Jews in Paul's day. Their salvation teetered on their frantic efforts to keep the Law of Moses. To prove the truth of what he was saying, Paul reached back in history past Moses to Abraham, the father of the Jews.

> What then shall we say that Abraham, our fore-father according to the flesh, has found? For if Abraham was justified by works, he has something to

---

2. How could a just God declare a guilty person innocent? God's justice was satisfied when Jesus took our sentence of death upon Himself. By punishing Christ for our sins, God could be both "just and the justifier of the one who has faith in Jesus" (v. 26).

boast about; but not before God. For what does the
Scripture say? "And Abraham believed God, and it
was reckoned to him as righteousness." (Rom. 4:1–3)

If Abraham had tried to work for his justification, he could have
compared himself with others and come out ahead. From the perspective of his peers, he was a good man and deserved God's favor.
But God doesn't operate by relative, human standards. Abraham's
works gained him no merit because, good as they were, they still
fell short of God's absolute, perfect measure.

So, according to Genesis, he simply put his faith in the One
who promised him the stars:

And He took him outside and said, "Now look toward
the heavens, and count the stars, if you are able to
count them." And He said to him, "So shall your de-
scendants be." Then he believed in the Lord; and
He reckoned it to him as righteousness. (Gen. 15:5–6)

Paul anchors his point on the word *reckoned*. It's a bookkeeper's
term that means "to credit to someone's account." Before meeting
God, Abraham's spiritual ledger showed nothing but debits. Then,
in one moment of faith, he went from a spiritual pauper to a
billionaire. The Lord canceled his sinful debts and credited his
account with His own perfect righteousness.

Clarification

Some might argue, however, that Abraham earned God's favor
by his faith. The problem with that view is this: you can't earn a
gift. If you work for something, it's a wage that's due you. Paul
explains:

Now to the one who works, his wage is not reckoned
as a favor, but as what is due. But to the one who
does not work, but believes in Him who justifies the
ungodly, his faith is reckoned as righteousness.
(Rom. 4:4–5)

God saves us purely by His grace. Christ pays our way into
heaven, and He gets all the credit. The only way we can receive
the gift of God's grace is if we do *not* work for it.

Just as David also speaks of the blessing upon the man
to whom God reckons righteousness apart from works:

"Blessed are those whose lawless deeds have been
forgiven,
And whose sins have been covered.
Blessed is the man whose sin the Lord will not
take into account."
(vv. 6–8; see also Ps. 32)

Do you know when David wrote these words? After his affair
with Bathsheba and murder of her husband, Uriah. He covered up
his sins for a year before finally being confronted by the prophet
Nathan. He then sought and received God's unmerited forgiveness.

You've heard of "do-it-yourself" kits. Salvation is a *"don't-do-it-
yourself"* kit. Don't touch it! Don't try to put it together yourself!
It's finished, like a new car fresh off the assembly line. We just settle
inside and enjoy the ride.

The Grace-Faith Transaction according to Ephesians

In the book of Ephesians, Paul puts forth another argument for
why we can't work our way into heaven. The reason here is
simple—dead people can't work.

> And you were dead in your trespasses and sins,
> in which you formerly walked according to the
> course of this world, according to the prince of the
> power of the air, of the spirit that is now working in
> the sons of disobedience. Among them we too all for-
> merly lived in the lusts of our flesh, indulging the
> desires of the flesh and of the mind, and were by
> nature children of wrath, even as the rest. (Eph. 2:1–3)

Without Christ, we're like Lazarus in the tomb—totally helpless. Impressive wrappings may adorn our bodies, but we are still
dead inside; no amount of religious decoration can bring us back
to life. We need help from a higher source.

Vertically

Verse 4 begins, "But God"—not "God and me" or "God and a
few of my good works" or "God and my money." God alone calls
us up from the grave.

> But God, being rich in mercy, because of His great
> love with which He loved us, even when we were

21

dead in our transgressions, made us alive together with Christ (by grace you have been saved), and raised us up with Him, and seated us with Him in the heavenly places, in Christ Jesus, in order that in the ages to come He might show the surpassing riches of His grace in kindness toward us in Christ Jesus. (vv. 4–7)

We are raised up with Christ, seated in the high heavenly places. Positionally, this is how God sees us—not debased but enthroned. What grace!

Grace is unmerited favor. It is "the kindness and love of God our Saviour toward man" (Titus 3:4). Love that goes upward is worship; love that goes outward is affection; love that stoops is grace.[3]

God finds us mired in sin, tossed aside, unlovely, and unlovable. With a sweeping gesture of love, He stoops down to us to take us in His arms. Our response is to reach up in faith.

Horizontally

For by grace you have been saved through faith; and that not of yourselves, it is the gift of God; not as a result of works, that no one should boast. (vv. 8–9)

We are saved as Abraham was saved: not by works but by taking God at His word and receiving His grace. Our relationships with one another are characterized by humility—since we've been saved by God's grace, we have nothing to boast about.

The Grace-Faith Transaction and Me

Three statements can summarize the grace-faith transaction between God and us: He demonstrates His love; I declare my need; I take His gift. One, two, three. Salvation is as simple as that.

Have you come to God loaded down with good deeds and religious accomplishments, hoping He will accept you because of them? One by one, let them fall from your arms, and let God lovingly place His gift of eternal life in your upturned and empty hands.

---

3. Donald Grey Barnhouse, *Man's Ruin* (Grand Rapids, Mich.: William B. Eerdmans Publishing Co., 1952), p. 72.

Living Insights

The Bible is a photo album filled with pictures of God's grace. One striking image waits for us in the pages of 2 Samuel. The setting is the palace of King David. Gold and bronze fixtures gleam from the walls. Lofty, wooden ceilings crown each spacious room. In the banquet room, David and his children gather for an evening meal. Absalom, tanned and handsome, is there, as is David's beautiful daughter Tamar. The call to dinner is given, and the king scans the room to see if all are present. One figure, though, is absent.

Clump, scraaape, clump, scraaape. The sound coming down the hall echoes into the chamber. *Clump, scraaape, clump, scraaape.* Finally, the person appears at the door and slowly shuffles to his seat. It is lame Mephibosheth. Now the feast can begin.

Mephibosheth is not one of David's sons. He is not even a member of David's royal line. Why does he eat at the King's table? Take a moment to read the whole account in 2 Samuel 9.

What did Mephibosheth do to earn David's favor?

_____

Why did David regard Mephibosheth as one of his sons?

_____

_____

From David's palace, we move to the golden banquet hall of heaven. The room radiates with the glory of God. The doors open, and masses of people enter. But instead of the mighty and handsome, in hobble the sick, the lame, and the disfigured—those whose lives have been broken by the crippling effects of sin (compare Luke 14:12–24).

Do you see yourself in this crowd? Maybe you are one of them, but you are still waiting outside the door. God is sending you an invitation sealed by the blood of Christ to come to His table. Won't you receive His grace and come in?

Let the following poem by Julie Martin help put your thoughts into words. Following the poem, we've provided some space for you to express your heart to the Lord.

Grace in a Barren Place

I was that Mephibosheth
Crippled by my twisted pride and
    hiding from You in a barren place
        where You could not find me
        where You would not give me what I
           deserved

But somehow You found me and
I don't understand why but You
    gave me what I *do not* deserve
You not only spared my desolate life but
    You made it bountiful
And here at Your table
I will thank You my
    King.[4]

My Thoughts to God

_____

_____

_____

_____

_____

_____

_____

_____

_____

_____

_____

4. Julie Martin, from the study guide *David . . . A Man after God's Own Heart,* coauthored by Julie Martin, from the Bible-teaching ministry of Charles R. Swindoll (Fullerton, Calif.: Insight for Living, 1988), pp. 98–99.

Chapter 4
THE CLASSIC BATTLE
Romans 6:1–14; 7:7–21

O n July 4, 1776, the United States declared its independence, based upon the principles of freedom and equality for all . . . all except the slave. It took almost a hundred years, one courageous president, and the Civil War to lift the yoke of slavery in America.

In his second inaugural address in 1865, only weeks before he was assassinated, Abraham Lincoln noted how strange it was

> that any men should dare to ask a just God's assistance in wringing their bread from the sweat of other men's faces.[1]

On New Year's Day, 1863, the Emancipation Proclamation had been publicly announced; but it wasn't until December 18, 1865, that the Thirteenth Amendment to the Constitution was officially adopted, abolishing slavery in the United States.

Though legally freed, many in the South continued to live as slaves. Shelby Foote, in his three-volume work on the Civil War, documents this unexpected reaction.

> [Most slaves] could repeat, with equal validity, what an Alabama slave had said in 1864 when asked what he thought of the Great Emancipator whose proclamation went into effect that year. "I don't know nothing bout Abraham Lincoln," he replied, "cep they say he sot us free. And I don't know nothing bout that neither."[2]

Precious blood was spilled to set those slaves free, yet some never left the plantations. Many of them stayed because they feared the uncertainty of freedom. How tragic, though, not to take the risk of living free.

This chapter has been partially adapted from "Emancipated? Then Live Like It!" from the study guide *The Grace Awakening*, coauthored by Ken Gire, from the Bible-teaching ministry of Charles R. Swindoll (Fullerton, Calif.: Insight for Living, 1990).

1. As quoted by Carl Sandburg in *Abraham Lincoln: The Prairie Years and the War Years*, one-volume edition (New York, N.Y.: Harcourt Brace Jovanovich, Publishers, 1982), p. 664.

2. Shelby Foote, *The Civil War: A Narrative* (New York, N.Y.: Random House, Vintage Books, 1974), vol. 3, p. 1045.

Even more tragic is the fact that precious blood was spilled at Calvary to set us free spiritually, yet many Christians still live as though enslaved to an old taskmaster—sin.

Reviewing Some Thoughts on Slavery

Before we focus on our daily battle with sin, let's examine three truths about our relationship with our old master.

First: *All of us were born in bondage to sin.* Romans 1–3 reveals the iron manacles of depravity binding every type of person—the pagan, the moralist, and the religious. Though this first truth is grim, the second is glorious.

Second: *A day came when Christ set us free.* Chapter 3 does not end in despair. Our Great Emancipator proclaimed our freedom when He rose from the dead and broke our chains of sin and death (vv. 21–26). Romans 5 reveals the benefits of our freedom and ushers us into the open spaces of God's mercy:

> Therefore having been justified by faith, we have peace with God through our Lord Jesus Christ, through whom also we have obtained our introduction by faith into this grace in which we stand; and we exult in hope of the glory of God. (vv. 1–2)

Third: *Many Christians still live as though they are enslaved.* Christ has won our freedom, declared us righteous, and changed our hearts; but tragically, our old nature still clings to a life of slavery to sin. In Romans 6:1–14, Paul gives us the courage and the know-how to break free.

Claiming Our Freedom over Sin: Romans 6

Romans 6 is the Christian's emancipation proclamation. Two groups of believers, though, don't live out the fullness of this freedom: those who don't claim their liberty and continue to live like slaves (vv. 1–14), and those who push their freedom too far and take advantage of their liberty (vv. 15–23). The first group nullifies grace; the second group abuses it.

To both, Paul stands up and protests: "May it never be!" (vv. 2, 15). The very thought of grace being treated this way horrifies the Apostle. He recoils and says, in essence, "Perish the thought!" Then he poses a question to them in verse 2: "How shall we who died to sin still live in it?"

Paul's point in Romans 6 is that the old sinful nature that once ruled over us has been ousted from office; what we must learn now is how to keep it from regaining power over our lives. He presents three action steps to do just that—*know, consider,* and *present.*

Know

Let's begin with what we are to know.

> Or do you not know that all of us who have been baptized into Christ Jesus have been baptized into His death? Therefore we have been buried with Him through baptism into death, in order that as Christ was raised from the dead through the glory of the Father, so we too might walk in newness of life. For if we have become united with Him in the likeness of His death, certainly we shall be also in the likeness of His resurrection, knowing this, that our old self was crucified with Him, that our body of sin might be done away with, that we should no longer be slaves to sin; for he who has died is freed from sin. Now if we have died with Christ, we believe that we shall also live with Him, knowing that Christ, having been raised from the dead, is never to die again; death no longer is master over Him. For the death that He died, He died to sin, once for all; but the life that He lives, He lives to God. (vv. 3–10)

The word *baptism* comes from the Greek root *baptizō*, which essentially means "identification." It was a term used in the first century for dipping a garment into dye and changing the color or "identity" of the cloth.[3]

When Christ died on the cross, He was dipped or baptized into death (see Luke 12:50). He rose from the grave, and His perishable body changed to an imperishable one (see 1 Cor. 15:42–49; 1 John 3:2). When we trust in the Savior for eternal life, we become dipped into His death and resurrection. Similarly, our identity changes (see 2 Cor. 5:17). We don't see it; we don't hear it; we don't feel it. But it changes nevertheless. His death to sin becomes our death to sin;

3. See J. Dwight Pentecost, *The Words and Works of Jesus Christ* (Grand Rapids, Mich.: Zondervan Publishing House, 1981), p. 83.

His awakening to a whole new realm of life becomes our awakening. Positionally, our old nature dies on the cross, and with it, its dominion over us (see Col. 2:12–15).

This doesn't mean we are free from the reality of sin's presence in our old nature, but its mastery and domination over us is null and void. We now have the power to choose not to sin, and a victorious walk begins with knowing this fact.

Consider

Once we know this, there is something we need to consider.

> Even so consider yourselves to be dead to sin, but alive to God in Christ Jesus. (Rom. 6:11)

To experience the freedom Christ has given us, we must transform our way of thinking (see 12:2). We must consider it to be true that, since we died with Christ, we are dead to sin's rule over our lives; and since we were raised with Christ, we are alive to God's power. "Therefore," Paul says,

> do not let sin reign in your mortal body that you should obey its lusts. (6:12)

Here's a thought that may blow you away: You don't have to sin every day. Those who are maturing in Christ, becoming increasingly aware of their life in the Savior, and living in the Spirit's power can live above the drag of sin longer than they've ever dreamed.

Now, because we're human, we'll never be sinless. But we can become more and more aware of our choices to avoid sin and become stronger at resisting it.

Present

Knowing the truth of our freedom and counting it as real brings us to our third crucial action step: present.

> And do not go on presenting the members of your body to sin as instruments of unrighteousness but present yourselves to God as those alive from the dead, and your members as instruments of righteousness to God. For sin shall not be master over you, for you are not under law, but under grace. (vv. 13–14)

Christ redeemed our bodies as well as our souls. With His blood He purchased all our members—our hands, feet, arms, legs, eyes, ears . . . everything. And He has set them apart and empowered them for His glory. "So," Paul says, "stop giving them to evil! Offer them to God as instruments of good."

Now Paul doesn't say this will be easy. Even though Christ has liberated us, the lifelong patterns and perspectives of our old nature are determined to keep us in bondage. If we hope to experience the full benefits of freedom, we must prepare for a classic battle. And there's no better place to observe the conflict than Romans 7.

Portrait of a Struggling Christian: Romans 7

In Romans 1–3, Paul showed us the lost person; in chapters 4–5, the justified person; in chapter 6, the victorious person. Suddenly, when we come to chapter 7, Paul turns inward and paints a self-portrait so stark and real it catches us off guard. "Wretched man that I am!" he cries out in frustration over his struggles with sin (7:24)—struggles we all can understand.

At the center of the conflict is God's law, which is good for us, on the one hand, because it defines the line between right and wrong. But it is bad for us, on the other hand, because it enlivens our sinful desires (see vv. 7–11). Who hasn't seen a Keep Off the Grass sign and not felt an urge to walk on the grass? That's our sin nature rearing up and, as Paul says, "taking opportunity through the commandment" (vv. 8, 11).

God's law is the catalyst that causes our new and old natures to fight against each other. We can feel the intense heat from the battle in Paul's life in verses 14–24:

> For we know that the Law is spiritual; but I am of flesh, sold into bondage to sin. For that which I am doing, I do not understand; for I am not practicing what I would like to do, but I am doing the very thing I hate. But if I do the very thing I do not wish to do, I agree with the Law, confessing that it is good. So now, no longer am I the one doing it, but sin which indwells me. For I know that nothing good dwells in me, that is, in my flesh; for the wishing is present in me, but the doing of the good is not. For the good that I wish, I do not do; but I practice the very evil that I do not wish. But if I am doing the very thing I do not wish, I am no longer the one doing it, but sin which dwells in me. I find then the

principle that evil is present in me, the one who wishes to do good. For I joyfully concur with the law of God in the inner man, but I see a different law in the members of my body, waging war against the law of my mind, and making me a prisoner of the law of sin which is in my members. Wretched man that I am! Who will set me free from the body of this death?

Thankfully, Paul's story does not end here. On the horizon is a shining word of hope in Romans 8: the presence and power of the Holy Spirit. In the meantime, we can lift a few principles from Paul's experience to help us survive our own war with sin.

Realistically, How Do We Survive?

His example gives us four survival tips. First, *freely say, "I don't understand."* That's what Paul said in verse 15. Admitting that you can't explain everything gives you permission to be human. It's OK not to know all the answers.

Second, *accept your own imperfections.* Paul said, "I know that nothing good dwells in me, that is, in my flesh; for the wishing is present in me, but the doing of the good is not" (v. 18). A healthy self-awareness helps us stay balanced. Don't make the ideal your standard, otherwise you'll continually feel defeated.

Third, *leave room for failure.* Paul acknowledged, "The good that I wish, I do not do; but I practice the very evil that I do not wish" (v. 19). If the great apostle Paul failed, should we expect any different for ourselves?

Fourth, *admit your true feelings to God.* God can handle our feelings. In fact, until we come to the point of honest repentance, we're not ready for the Holy Spirit's power in our lives. We're not ready for ultimate victory.

 Living Insights

Do you remember Hans Christian Andersen's tale of *The Ugly Duckling*? From the day he hatched, the other animals criticized him. "You're ugly," they pecked, pointing out all his flaws. The poor little duckling believed their lies and was very unhappy. One despairing day, he saw some swans gliding across the water and was overwhelmed by their grace. Coming near them, he saw his reflection in the water and at once realized he was a swan too! That truth transformed him forever. Spreading his beautiful white wings, he shook off his former shame and joined the flock of swans, never to return to the other animals.

Jesus said to His followers,

> "If you abide in My word, then you are truly disciples of Mine; and you shall know the truth, and the truth shall make you free." (John 8:31–32)

Do you know the truth about who you are in Christ? Have you experienced truth's freedom? Have you been able to shake off the fear, shame, and guilt of your past? Take a few minutes to look at your reflection in the following verses and write down what you see. Begin each statement with "I am . . ."

John 1:12 _____

_____

John 8:36 _____

_____

John 15:15 _____

_____

1 Corinthians 3:16 _____

_____

1 Corinthians 6:20 _____

_____

Galatians 5:1 _____

_____

Ephesians 2:10 _____

_____

Philippians 3:20 _____

Colossians 2:9–10 _____

1 Peter 2:9–10 _____

Jude 1 _____

Do you see the swan in the water now? How does this new
knowledge about yourself affect your choices and actions?

_____

_____

_____

_____

_____

_____

_____

_____

_____

_____

_____

_____

_____

_____

_____

_____

Chapter 5

THE CLASSIC VICTORY
Romans 8:1–17, 31–39

R omans 8 is without doubt one of the best-known, best-loved chapters of the Bible," writes commentator John R. W. Stott.[1] It is the ray of sunshine breaking through the stormy clouds of Romans 7, the hopeful answer to Paul's desperate cry: "Wretched man that I am! Who will set me free from the body of this death?" (v. 24).

In one sense, Paul has answered that question already in Romans 6. Christ bought our freedom from sin through His death on the cross (see vv. 5–7). Yet, as much as we wish to live free from our old master, our fleshly nature still pulls us to do evil. The tug-of-war within our hearts rages, with the flesh too often gaining the upper hand. The Law can't help us gain victory over sin. And we can't get victory ourselves. Who will come to our rescue?

Thankfully, our divine Helper arrives in Romans 8. Stott explains:

> If in Romans 7 Paul has been preoccupied with the place of the law, in Romans 8 his preoccupation is with the work of the Spirit. . . . The essential contrast which Paul paints is between the weakness of the law and the power of the Spirit. For over against indwelling sin, which is the reason the law is unable to help us in our moral struggle (7:17, 20), Paul now sets the indwelling Spirit, who is both our liberator now from "the law of sin and death" (8:2) and the guarantee of resurrection and eternal glory in the end (8:11, 17, 23). Thus the Christian life is essentially life in the Spirit, that is to say, a life which is animated, sustained, directed and enriched by the Holy Spirit. Without the Holy Spirit true Christian discipleship would be inconceivable, indeed impossible.[2]

The key to victory over sin, then, is living in the Spirit. Let's look to Romans 8 for insight into what that means.

---

1. John Stott, *Romans: God's Good News for the World* (Downers Grove, Ill.: InterVarsity Press, 1994), p. 216.

2. Stott, *Romans*, p. 216.

Justification: Alive in Christ

Before we can learn what living in the Spirit means, we must first be firmly rooted in what being saved by Christ does for us. Three foundational truths are crucial to understand: (1) we are eternally secure, (2) we are internally freed, and (3) we are positionally perfect.

We Are Eternally Secure

> There is therefore now no condemnation for
> those who are in Christ Jesus. (8:1)

What a promise! No longer are we condemned by our sins, fearing hell as our just punishment. God has removed the sword of condemnation dangling over our heads and replaced it with a crown of eternal life—a gift we have neither earned nor deserved. Had we earned eternal life, keeping it would depend on us. But since God gave us this gift, our security rests in Him. He has placed us "in Christ Jesus," and no one can snatch us out of His hands (see John 10:27–30).

We Are Internally Freed

> For the law of the Spirit of life in Christ Jesus has set
> you free from the law of sin and of death. (Rom. 8:2)

The word *for* points to the reason God no longer condemns us: we are "free from the law of sin and of death." You see, before we were saved, each violation of God's law forged a link in sin's chain dragging us down . . . down . . . down to destruction. We strained against it with all our might, but no mere human is strong enough to resist death's relentless pull.

When God places us in Christ, however, He enacts a new law of life that breaks the chain of sin. We're free! Destruction is no longer our destiny—eternal life in paradise is. Therefore we can face eternity without fear, knowing that when our bodies go into the grave, our souls will fly to heaven.

We Are Positionally Perfect

> For what the Law could not do, weak as it was
> through the flesh, God did: sending His own Son
> in the likeness of sinful flesh and as an offering for
> sin, He condemned sin in the flesh, in order that

the requirement of the Law might be fulfilled in us, who do not walk according to the flesh, but according to the Spirit. (vv. 3–4)

The reason for our freedom, once again, is not the Law. The Law can't free us, because it depends on our ability to obey it, and that ability is desperately weak. So God did what no code of conduct could do: He sent Jesus to keep the Law for us. Then He offered His precious Son on the altar of the cross, laying on Him the sentence of death that the Law demanded of us.

God considers the Law's requirement fulfilled in us by virtue of our position in Christ, who fulfilled the Law completely. In Christ, we are justified—declared perfect. God has replaced our sinfulness with Christ's perfection. And one day God promises to present us before His throne "in the presence of His glory blameless with great joy" (Jude 24).

Just think . . . the very identity of Christ resides within us. This concept can transform the way we view ourselves, the way we see others, the way we approach our lives. Here's the key to remember: Jesus died on the cross to *change* our lives, not just to save us. Justification should always lead to sanctification—the process by which the indwelling Spirit produces in us the life of Christ.

Sanctification: Living in the Spirit

What does a Spirit-empowered life look like? Let's go on to the next section of Romans 8, where Paul highlights its beauty against the dark backdrop of life lived in the flesh.

> For those who are according to the flesh set their minds on the things of the flesh, but those who are according to the Spirit, the things of the Spirit. For the mind set on the flesh is death, but the mind set on the Spirit is life and peace, because the mind set on the flesh is hostile toward God; for it does not subject itself to the law of God, for it is not even able to do so; and those who are in the flesh cannot please God. However, you are not in the flesh but in the Spirit, if indeed the Spirit of God dwells in you. But if anyone does not have the Spirit of Christ, he does not belong to Him. And if Christ is in you, though the body is dead because of sin, yet the spirit

is alive because of righteousness. But if the Spirit of Him who raised Jesus from the dead dwells in you, He who raised Christ Jesus from the dead will also give life to your mortal bodies through His Spirit who indwells you. (vv. 5–11)

These two lifestyles are as opposite as January and July. Notice their stark differences in the following chart.

Life according to the Flesh	Life according to the Spirit
Flesh-oriented mind-set (v. 5a)	Spirit-oriented mind-set (v. 5b)
Deathlike existence (v. 6a)	Vital, life-and-peace experience (v. 6b)
Hostility toward God (v. 7a)	Spirit-indwelt life (v. 9)
Rebellious attitude (v. 7b)	Spiritually alive (v. 10)
Inability to obey or please God (vv. 7b–8)	Resurrection power (v. 11)

Our options seem clear, don't they? We can either give control to the Spirit who dwells within us, or we can try to please God with our own efforts. That would be like accepting His saving grace by faith but then going back to earning His favor by works. As Paul wrote to the Galatians, "Having begun by the Spirit, are you now being perfected by the flesh?" (Gal. 3:3). It's ridiculous—isn't it?

Choosing the Spirit over our flesh sounds like a simple choice, but for many Christians, it's not an easy one. We're used to doing everything ourselves. Our addiction to working for our salvation doesn't vanish the moment we accept God's gift of eternal life. In fact, we feel obligated to work *extra* hard to please God now that we're saved.[3]

But Paul's point is this: we won't know what living is all about until we start living by the Spirit (Rom. 8:13b). This means changing our everything-depends-on-me attitude to a mind-set of dependency that says, "He can accomplish what I can't. He's in control."

---

3. Paul reassures us that we are not under obligation "to the flesh, to live according to the flesh" (Rom. 8:12). We don't have to repay a pound of grace with a pound of works. Trying to please God in the flesh invariably leads to pride and a whole host of deadly sins. Paul warns us, "If you are living according to the flesh, you must die"—you will experience a deathlike existence spiritually. On the other hand, if we live in the Spirit, He will help us shed our fleshly sins so we can experience life to the fullest (v. 13).

What can the Spirit accomplish when we rest in His power? Romans 8 gives us the beginning of an incredible list.

1. He gives us the fruit of His presence:

   The mind set on the Spirit is life and peace. (v. 6b)

2. He enables us to put to death the fleshly sins that control our lives:

   If by the Spirit you are putting to death the deeds of the body, you will live. (v. 13b)

3. He leads us:

   For all who are being led by the Spirit of God, these are sons of God. (v. 14)

4. He removes our fear and reassures us that we are God's children:

   For you have not received a spirit of slavery leading to fear again, but you have received a spirit of adoption as sons by which we cry out, "Abba! Father!" The Spirit Himself bears witness with our spirit that we are children of God. (vv. 15–16)

5. He strengthens us by interceding in prayer for us:

   And in the same way the Spirit also helps our weakness; for we do not know how to pray as we should, but the Spirit Himself intercedes for us with groanings too deep for words; and He who searches the hearts knows what the mind of the Spirit is, because He intercedes for the saints according to the will of God. (vv. 26–27)

6. He gives us a foretaste of our future inheritance in glory:

   If children, heirs also, heirs of God and fellow heirs with Christ, if indeed we suffer with Him in order that we may also be glorified with Him. . . . And not only this, but also we ourselves, having the first fruits of the Spirit, even we ourselves groan within ourselves, waiting eagerly for our adoption as sons, the redemption of our body. (vv. 17, 23)

Glorification: Eternally in God's Presence

First we receive justification. Then we experience the lifelong process of sanctification. And finally, we reach glorification, where our mortality puts on immortality and we enter God's presence forever (see vv. 28–30; 1 Cor. 15:50–57).

In Paul's final passage in Romans 8, he not only gives us a glimpse of that glory, but he assembles all the subjects that he has been developing so far: our helplessness, God's grace, Christ's sacrifice, our justification, the assurance of our salvation, the sanctifying power of the Holy Spirit. Like a mighty crescendo, these ideas build and build, until one triumphant theme soars above them all—the victorious power of God's love.

> What then shall we say to these things? If God is for us, who is against us? He who did not spare His own Son, but delivered Him up for us all, how will He not also with Him freely give us all things? Who will bring a charge against God's elect? God is the one who justifies; who is the one who condemns? Christ Jesus is He who died, yes, rather who was raised, who is at the right hand of God, who also intercedes for us. Who shall separate us from the love of Christ? Shall tribulation, or distress, or persecution, or famine, or nakedness, or peril, or sword? Just as it is written,
>
> "For Thy sake we are being put to death
> all day long;
> We were considered as sheep to be
> slaughtered."
>
> But in all these things we overwhelmingly conquer through Him who loved us. For I am convinced that neither death, nor life, nor angels, nor principalities, nor things present, nor things to come, nor powers, nor height, nor depth, nor any other created thing, shall be able to separate us from the love of God, which is in Christ Jesus our Lord. (vv. 31–39)

Every Christian doctrine draws its life's blood from the love of God. It is the heart of the classic gospel.

Living Insights

"Connection to Chicago, Gate 31," the flight attendant reads to you from her clipboard. Glancing at her watch, she adds, "Departing in ten minutes. You'd better hurry."

You sling one carry-on over your shoulder and gather up two others. As you set out, you notice the sign above your head: Gate 3. *Oh, boy.* A wave of panic swells from your feet into your chest, pushing up your heart rate and making your face flush.

You wade into the stream of people and start swimming with the current. Already, though, you feel the drag on your arms. Gate 5. *Why don't they put these connecting flights closer together?*

You're walking as fast as you can without jogging. You try to do that too, but you quickly get winded and have to pull back to a swift walk. A bead of sweat trickles down the side of your face. On the right, an airport clock appears. *Five minutes!* Gate 10.

Just then, you see something ahead that gives you a glimmer of hope. A moving sidewalk! As you step onto the black ribbon, new energy surges through you. You walk at the same pace as before, but the rubber belt whisks you along at twice the speed. Gate 18 . . . Gate 23 . . . Gate 27. Pictures pass by in a blur. A cool breeze flows against your face. *Now I'm getting somewhere!*

Finally, the sidewalk comes to an end. Stepping off feels like shifting from overdrive into low gear. Your feet keep moving, but the world has slipped into slow motion. It doesn't matter. Here's Gate 31. *Whew.* Just in time for final boarding.

Settling into your seat, you catch your breath and think about the freedom you experienced on the moving sidewalk. You smile, *Now that's what I call power walking!*

◆

Living by the Spirit is a lot like walking on that moving sidewalk. We're moving—using our gifts, exercising our faith, confronting the sin in our lives—but the Spirit is doubling, even tripling our efforts. We feel His power beneath our feet, energizing every step.

Living according to the flesh is like stepping off the fast-moving belt into a pit of sand. Our feet feel like lead. Every step forward requires great effort, and we don't see much change in our lives.

In Romans 8:26–27, Paul shows us the entrance to the Spirit's moving sidewalk: prayer. How does the Holy Spirit multiply the effectiveness of our prayers?

_____

_____

Lately, have you been straining in the flesh to move forward in any of these areas?

- improving a relationship
- overcoming a self-defeating habit
- learning a ministry skill
- helping someone grow in the Lord
- other _____

Make a plan concerning this area to step onto God's power belt through prayer. List some items to pray for and when you're going to pray for them.

_____

_____

_____

_____

_____

_____

The choice is yours. You can walk in your own strength, puffing and sweating and getting nowhere. Or you can walk in the Spirit and feel the wind in your face and the ground moving beneath your feet. Which will it be?

Chapter 6

THE CLASSIC SACRIFICE

Romans 12:1–3

Shoulders hunched, the man plods through life, straining with every step to carry the great burden bound to his back. It has been his night-and-day companion. Not once has he known relief from its merciless weight.

The man's name is Christian, the central character in John Bunyan's classic allegory *The Pilgrim's Progress*. In one moving scene from the book, Christian finds the path to salvation. Up the hill he staggers until he reaches the peak. There he sees a wooden cross and, just below it, an empty sepulcher. As he nears the cross, a miracle happens. The straps binding the massive weight to his shoulders loosen, and his load tumbles away into the sepulcher's waiting mouth, never to be seen again.

A delicious feeling of lightness buoys Christian's body, and joyous tears of relief stream down his face. Three Shining Ones then approach him. The first announces, "Thy Sins be forgiven"; the second strips away his rags and dresses him in splendid clothes; the third hands him a sealed scroll, which he is to present upon entrance to the Celestial City.

Overwhelmed by his new freedom, Christian sings:

> Thus far did I come laden with my Sin;
> Nor could ought ease the grief that I was in,
> Till I came hither: What a place is this!
> Must here be the beginning of my bliss?
> Must here the Burden fall from off my back?
> Must here the strings that bound it to me crack?
> Blest Cross! blest Sepulchre! blest rather be
> The *Man* that there was put to Shame for me![1]

In this brief scene, Bunyan has eloquently dramatized the message of Romans. We all are pilgrims, encumbered by a crushing load of sin. When we stumble to the Cross, God releases our burdens, burying them forever in Christ's own grave. He proclaims us forgiven

---

1. John Bunyan, *The Pilgrim's Progress* (Uhrichsville, Ohio: Barbour and Company, 1985), p. 36.

and drapes us in a new identity as His children. Then He places in our hands a passport to heaven, sealed by the Holy Spirit Himself.

Such love! Such relentless grace! How can we respond? Isaac Watts answered that question in the final verse of his hymn "When I Survey the Wondrous Cross":

> Were the whole realm of nature mine,
> That were a present far too small;
> Love so amazing, so divine,
> Demands my soul, my life, my all.[2]

Love's Response

Divine love does what the Law could never do: It moves us to the point of personal sacrifice. Laws and rules may change our behavior, but only love can change our hearts. If God simply wanted our compliance, He could have torn back the veil of heaven, let His unrefracted glory blaze, and frightened us into obedience. Instead, He opened His heart, gave us His Son, and sought to win our love.

In the first few verses of Romans 12, Paul reveals three ways we can open our hearts in return: consecration, transformation, and self-evaluation. Let's enter into them one at a time.

Consecration

> I urge you therefore, brethren, by the mercies of God, to present your bodies a living and holy sacrifice, acceptable to God, which is your spiritual service of worship. (v. 1)

The word *therefore* flags an important transition of thought in Paul's epistle. This is actually the third great *therefore* in the book.

- The first appeared in 5:1—"Therefore having been justified by faith." *Salvation* was the key idea in this section, flowing out of the themes of sin and grace in chapters 1–4.

- The second *therefore* appeared in chapter 8: "There is therefore now no condemnation for those who are in Christ Jesus" (v. 1). The central theme here was *security*. Not only does God save us, He seals us. He gives us the Holy Spirit both as a pledge of

---

2. Isaac Watts, "When I Survey the Wondrous Cross," in *Hymns for the Family of God* (Nashville, Tenn.: Paragon Associates, 1976), no. 258.

a heavenly future and a promise of power to live for Christ.

Building on these mighty pillars of truth, Paul constructs a framework of *service* in Romans 12. He begins by pleading for our commitment to Christ: "I *urge* you therefore, brethren." Divine love may call to our hearts, but Christ won't force our devotion. The choice and responsibility are ours.

The word *brethren* means us—those whose sins have been forgiven, whose burdens have been lifted, whose thirst has been quenched at the cool springs of God's mercy. Because we have received so much, Paul implores us to consecrate ourselves to Him: "Present your bodies a living and holy sacrifice." Someone has quipped, "The problem with living sacrifices is they keep crawling off the altar." In spite of our vacillating nature, God accepts us. He wants us to give ourselves to Him just as we are. In *The Message*, Eugene Peterson paraphrases Paul's command,

> Take your everyday, ordinary life—your sleeping, eating, going-to-work, and walking-around life— and place it before God as an offering.[3]

Martyrs sacrifice themselves by dying for a cause. God wants us to sacrifice ourselves by *living* for Him. This is not a one-time decision, like salvation. It is a day-by-day, moment-by-moment resolution. We keep on giving Him our eyes, ears, hands, feet, and lips to use for His purposes.

Transformation

The path of consecration leads to a changed life. In verse 2, Paul tells us what kind of change should take place by giving us a negative and a positive command:

> And do not be conformed to this world, but be transformed by the renewing of your mind, that you may prove what the will of God is, that which is good and acceptable and perfect. (v. 2)

Don't be *conformed*, he says first. The word comes from the Greek root *suschēmatizō*, which, according to scholar Kenneth Wuest,

> refers to the act of an individual assuming an outward

---

3. Eugene H. Peterson, *The Message: The New Testament in Contemporary English* (Colorado Springs, Colo.: NavPress, 1993), p. 328.

expression that does not come from within him, nor is it representative of his inner heart life. . . . Paul exhorts the saints, "Stop assuming an outward expression which is patterned after this world, an expression which does not come from, nor is it representative of what you are in your inner being as a regenerated child of God."[4]

The idea is this: Don't wear a mask of worldly habits, expressions, goals, perspectives, and opinions that hides the true nature of Christ within you. "Instead of masquerading in the habiliments of this age," Wuest continues,

> Paul exhorts the saints to be transformed. The word is *metamorphoomai*, which speaks of the act of a person changing his outward expression from that which he has to a different one, an expression which comes from and is representative of his inner being.[5]

Transformation doesn't mean changing into someone different— it's becoming who we really are in Christ. Jesus Himself illustrates this truth for us in the Transfiguration (see Matt. 17:2; Mark 9:2–3). When He was transfigured (the same word in Greek as *transformed*), He allowed "the glory of the essence of His deity that came from His inner being as deity . . . to shine through His human body."[6] In that moment, the reality of His eternal nature shone through His time-bound mortal body.

What we learn from Christ and Paul, then, is to yield to the Spirit as He leads us in a lifestyle consistent with our redeemed, eternal nature. We are now citizens of heaven, and we need to learn how to live like it (see Eph. 2:19; Phil. 3:20–21).

How, specifically, can we do this? Paul urges us to "be transformed by the renewing of your mind" (Rom. 12:2). We reshape our attitudes and perspectives through the power of God's Word, which can penetrate to the inner parts of our being (Heb. 4:12);

---

4. Kenneth S. Wuest, *Romans in the Greek New Testament* (Grand Rapids, Mich.: William B. Eerdmans Publishing Co., 1955), pp. 206–7.

5. Wuest, *Romans in the Greek New Testament*, p. 207.

6. Wuest, *Romans in the Greek New Testament*, p. 207. Another way to look at being transformed is through the prism of the marriage relationship. Two people are not converted into one the moment they say, "I do." Rather, they slowly become one through melding their goals, decisions, and lives in the dailiness of their relationship.

and also with the power of the Holy Spirit, who not only leads us but renews our spirits at salvation (Titus 3:5).

The change in our thinking will be nothing less than radical, and the results will show without doubt how "good and acceptable and perfect" God's will is (Rom. 12:2).

Self-Evaluation

In verse 3, Paul shifts from our relationship to God to our relationships with ourselves and others:

> For through the grace given to me I say to every man among you not to think more highly of himself than he ought to think; but to think so as to have sound judgment, as God has allotted to each a measure of faith.

That's good counsel, isn't it? Don't have an inflated opinion of yourself. But don't think too lowly of yourself either, treating yourself without respect, believing you're worthless. Rather, have "sound judgment"—that is, be realistic about who you are, know your gifts, and use them to minister to others (see vv. 4–8).

Three Things to Sacrifice

The divine altar is waiting for our sacrifice. What can we place on it?

First, we can sacrifice our *wills*. Have you ever seen a farmer try to move a mule when it doesn't want to budge? He pushes and pulls and throws his hat on the ground, but the mule just sits there. God must feel just as exasperated when we don't sacrifice our wills to Him. He may try to pull us away from a destructive lifestyle or an unhealthy relationship, but we stiffen our necks and refuse to follow. Sacrificing our wills means submitting to Him, being teachable, and being sensitive to His will. How easy are you to lead?

Second, we can sacrifice our *ways*. Are we available to go wherever God wants us to go? Are we willing to change our direction in life? Abraham was. He obeyed God's call and "went out, not knowing where he was going" (Heb. 11:8). To what new land is God leading you? The ministry, perhaps? More education? A different career? A new city? A commitment in a relationship?

Third, we can sacrifice our *words*. Not just the type of words but our verbosity. Frankly, most of us talk too much. We're constantly stuffing words into the gaps in our lives. Silence is perhaps the most precious yet neglected discipline in our daily walk. In his searching book *The Way of the Heart*, Henri Nouwen explains why:

> One of our main problems is that in this chatty society, silence has become a very fearful thing. For most people, silence creates itchiness and nervousness. Many experience silence not as full and rich, but as empty and hollow. For them silence is like a gaping abyss which can swallow them up. As soon as a minister says during a worship service, "Let us be silent for few moments," people tend to become restless and preoccupied with only one thought: "When will this be over?"[7]

Does silence make *you* anxious and fidgety? The psalmist bids us, "Be still, and know that I am God" (Ps. 46:10a KJV). By sacrificing our words, we're able to point people "beyond our words to the unspeakable mystery of God."[8]

And what better place can we bring them to?

 Living Insights STUDY ONE

The appetite of God's altar seems never to be satisfied. I place my weekend on the cold stone, and it craves my whole week. I offer it my house, and it wants my family. I toss it a few dollars, and it calls for my life's savings. It will not give up until it has consumed me, body and soul.

And then I will have nothing.

Really? The apostle Paul poured himself on God's altar. According to Philippians 3:4–11, what did he gain in return?

_____

_____

_____

Jesus came that we "might have life, and might have it abundantly" (John 10:10b). What path did He say will lead us to that

7. Henri J. M. Nouwen, *The Way of the Heart* (New York, N.Y.: Ballantine Books, 1981), p. 43.

8. Nouwen, *The Way of the Heart*, p. 43.

fullness of life (see Luke 9:23–25)?

_____

_____

_____

Amazing, isn't it? We die so we can live, empty ourselves to become full, let go of what is precious to gain what is eternal.

Have you placed your life on God's altar? Are you ready to sacrifice your will, your way, and your words in order to gain His will, His way, and His words?

To help kindle your spirit, meditate on the following prayer by Thomas à Kempis. If his words express the desires of your heart, let his prayer become your own and send it flying toward heaven as the first sparks of your sacrificed life.

> Almighty God,
> You who have made all things for me,
>   and me for your glory,
> Sanctify my body and soul,
> My thoughts and my intentions,
> My words and actions,
> That whatsoever I shall think,
>   or speak,
>   or do,
> May by me be designed to the glorification of your
>   name.
>
> And let no pride or self-seeking,
>   no impure motive or unworthy purpose,
>   no little ends or low imagination
> Stain my spirit, or
> Profane any of my words and actions.
>
> But let my body be a servant to my spirit,
> And both body and spirit
> Servants of Jesus Christ.[9]

9. Thomas à Kempis (adapted prayer), as quoted in *The One Year Book of Personal Prayer* (Wheaton, Ill.: Tyndale House Publishers, 1991), p. 260.

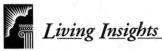

Stolen! All their money is gone, and they are in a foreign country. For a moment the couple panics; then they remember their American Express card. Whew! The commercial ends with the announcer's somber warning: "Don't leave home without it."

The world is an unpredictable place, so it's important that we carry some security in our pockets. For Christians traveling through the "foreign land" of an unsaved world, it's just as vital to carry the basic truths of the Christian faith—truths like the ones we studied in Romans. We'll reach for them again and again as we face threatening situations in our world.

Take a few moments to summarize the principles you learned from each chapter. Slip these points in your mental pocket along with the verses that follow each one. You'll be glad you didn't leave home without them!

The Classic Gospel

_____

_____

_____

> For I am not ashamed of the gospel, for it is the power of God for salvation to everyone who believes, to the Jew first and also to the Greek. For in it the righteousness of God is revealed from faith to faith; as it is written, "But the righteous man shall live by faith." (1:16–17)

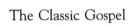

The Classic Problem

_____

_____

_____

For all have sinned and fall short of the glory of God. (3:23)

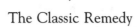

The Classic Remedy

_____

_____

_____

Now to the one who works, his wage is not reckoned as a favor, but as what is due. But to the one who does not work, but believes in Him who justifies the ungodly, his faith is reckoned as righteousness. . . . Therefore having been justified by faith, we have peace with God through our Lord Jesus Christ. (4:4–5; 5:1)

The Classic Battle

_____

_____

_____

For I know that nothing good dwells in me, that is, in my flesh; for the wishing is present in me, but the doing of the good is not. For the good that I wish, I do not do; but I practice the very evil that I do not wish. (7:18–19)

The Classic Victory

_____

_____

_____

But if the Spirit of Him who raised Jesus from the

dead dwells in you, He who raised Christ Jesus from the dead will also give life to your mortal bodies through His Spirit who indwells you. (8:11)

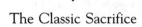

The Classic Sacrifice

I urge you therefore, brethren, by the mercies of God, to present your bodies a living and holy sacrifice, acceptable to God, which is your spiritual service of worship. And do not be conformed to this world, but be transformed by the renewing of your mind, that you may prove what the will of God is, that which is good and acceptable and perfect. (12:1–2)

BOOKS FOR PROBING FURTHER

*C*lassic.' A book which people praise and don't read."[1] Mark Twain's humor always had the bite of truth, didn't it? We hope his quip won't be true for you concerning the book of Romans. Though a classic, it should be praised but also read—and read often—because it unfolds for us the great mystery of God's grace.

If this brief study of the themes in Romans has whet your appetite for more of Paul's letter, please dig in! The following books elaborate on his thoughts and will supply a more comprehensive look at Romans as a whole.

Above all, let your study transform your life into a classic that will be read by those around you and inspire generations to come.

Barnhouse, Donald Grey. *Man's Ruin: Romans 1:1–32* (1952); and *God's Wrath: Romans 2:1–3:20* (1953). Two volumes in one. Reprint, Grand Rapids, Mich.: William B. Eerdmans Publishing Co., 1988. Volume 1.

———. *God's Remedy: Romans 3:21–4:25* (1954); and *God's River: Romans 5:1–11* (1959). Two volumes in one. Reprint, Grand Rapids, Mich.: William B. Eerdmans Publishing Co., 1988. Volume 2.

———. *God's Grace: Romans 5:12–21* (1959); *God's Freedom: Romans 6:1–7:25* (1961); and *God's Heirs: Romans 8:1–39* (1963). Three volumes in one. Reprint, Grand Rapids, Mich.: William B. Eerdmans Publishing Co., 1988. Volume 3.

———. *God's Covenants: Romans 9:1–11:36* (1963); *God's Discipline: Romans 12:1–14:12* (1964); and *God's Glory: Romans 14:13–16:27* (1964). Three volumes in one. Reprint, Grand Rapids, Mich.: William B. Eerdmans Publishing Co., 1988. Volume 4.

Christenson, Evelyn. *Gaining through Losing*. Wheaton, Ill.: Scripture Press Publications, Victor Books, 1980.

---

1. Mark Twain, as quoted in *Bartlett's Familiar Quotations*, 15th ed., rev. and enl., ed. Emily Morison Beck (Boston, Mass.: Little, Brown and Co., 1980), p. 625.

Graham, Billy. *Peace with God*. Rev. and exp. ed. Waco, Tex.: Word Books Publisher, 1984.

Macaulay, Ranald, and Jerram Barrs. *Being Human: The Nature of Spiritual Experience*. Downers Grove, Ill.: InterVarsity Press, 1978.

Morris, Leon. *Glory in the Cross: A Study in Atonement*. 1966. Reprint, Grand Rapids, Mich.: Baker Book House, 1979.

Pentecost, J. Dwight. *Designed to Be Like Him: Fellowship, Conduct, Conflict, Maturity*. Chicago, Ill.: Moody Press, 1966. Formerly titled *Pattern for Maturity*.

Stott, John R. W. *Basic Christianity*. 2d ed. Downers Grove, Ill.: InterVarsity Press, 1971.

————. *Romans: God's Good News for the World*. Downers Grove, Ill.: InterVarsity Press, 1994.

Swindoll, Charles R. *Growing Deep in the Christian Life: Returning to Our Roots*. Portland, Oreg.: Multnomah Press, 1986.

Some of these books may be out of print and available only through a library. For those currently available, please contact your local Christian bookstore. Books by Charles R. Swindoll may be obtained through Insight for Living. IFL also offers some books by other authors—please note the ordering information that follows and contact the office that serves you.

ORDERING INFORMATION

CLASSIC TRUTHS FOR TRIUMPHANT LIVING
Cassette Tapes and Study Guide

This Bible study guide was designed to be used independently or in conjunction with the broadcast of Chuck Swindoll's taped messages which are listed below. If you would like to order cassette tapes or further copies of this study guide, please see the information given below and the order forms provided at the end of this guide.

		U.S.	Canada
CTT	Study guide	$ 4.95 ea.	$ 6.50 ea.
CTTCS	Cassette series, includes all individual tapes, album cover, and one complimentary study guide	22.00	31.50 ea.
CTT 1–3	Individual cassettes, includes messages A and B	6.00 ea.	7.48 ea.

The prices are subject to change without notice.

CTT   1-A: *The Classic Gospel*—Romans 1:1, 7–17
       B: *The Classic Problem*—Romans 1:18–32

CTT   2-A: *The Classic Remedy**—Romans 4:1–8; Ephesians 2:1–9
       B: *The Classic Battle*—Romans 6:1–14; 7:7–21

CTT   3-A: *The Classic Victory*—Romans 8:1–17, 31–39
       B: *The Classic Sacrifice*—Romans 12:1–3

*This message was not a part of the original series but is compatible with it.

How to Order by Phone or FAX
(Credit card orders only)

United States: 1-800-772-8888 from 6:00 A.M. to 4:30 P.M., Pacific time, Monday through Friday
FAX (714) 575-5496 anytime, day or night

Canada: 1-800-663-7639, Vancouver residents call (604) 532-7172 from 8:00 A.M. to 4:30 P.M., Pacific time, Monday through Friday
FAX (604) 532-7173 anytime, day or night

Australia and the South Pacific: (03) 9-872-4606 or FAX (03) 9-874-8890
from 8:00 A.M. to 5:00 P.M., Monday through Friday

Other International Locations: call the Ordering Services Department
in the United States at (714) 575-5000 during the hours listed above.

How to Order by Mail

United States
• Mail to: Processing Services Department
   Insight for Living
   Post Office Box 69000
   Anaheim, CA 92817-0900
• Sales tax: California residents add 7.25%.
• Shipping and handling charges must be added to each order. See chart
on order form for amount.
• Payment: personal checks, money orders, credit cards (Visa, Master-
Card, Discover Card, and American Express). No invoices or COD orders
available.
• $10 fee for *any* returned check.

Canada
• Mail to: Insight for Living Ministries
   Post Office Box 2510
   Vancouver, BC V6B 3W7
• Sales tax: please add 7% GST. British Columbia residents also add 7%
sales tax (on tapes or cassette series).
• Shipping and handling charges must be added to each order. See chart
on order form for amount.
• Payment: personal cheques, money orders, credit cards (Visa, Master-
Card). No invoices or COD orders available.
• Delivery: approximately four weeks.

Australia and the South Pacific
• Mail to: Insight for Living, Inc.
   GPO Box 2823 EE
   Melbourne, Victoria 3001, Australia
• Shipping: add 25% to the total order.
• Delivery: approximately four to six weeks.
• Payment: personal checks payable in Australian funds, international
money orders, or credit cards (Visa, MasterCard, and BankCard).

Other International Locations
- Mail to: Processing Services Department
  Insight for Living
  Post Office Box 69000
  Anaheim, CA 92817-0900
- Shipping and delivery time: please see chart that follows.
- Payment: personal checks payable in U.S. funds, international money orders, or credit cards (Visa, MasterCard, and American Express).

Type of Shipping	Postage Cost	Delivery
Surface	10% of total order*	6 to 10 weeks
Airmail	25% of total order*	under 6 weeks

*Use U.S. price as a base.

Our Guarantee

Your complete satisfaction is our top priority here at Insight for Living. If you're not completely satisfied with anything you order, please return it for full credit, a refund, or a replacement, as *you* prefer.

Insight for Living Catalog

The Insight for Living catalog features study guides, tapes, and books by a variety of Christian authors. To obtain a free copy, call us at the numbers listed above.

Order Form
United States, Australia, and Other International Locations
(Canadian residents please use order form on reverse side.)

CTTCS represents the entire *Classic Truths for Triumphant Living* series in a special album cover, while CTT 1–3 are the individual tapes included in the series. CTT represents this study guide, should you desire to order additional copies.

CTT	Study guide	$ 4.95 ea.
CTTCS	Cassette series, includes all individual tapes, album cover, and one complimentary study guide	22.00
CTT 1–3	Individual cassettes, includes messages A and B	6.00 ea.

Product Code	Product Description	Quantity	Unit Price	Total
			$	$

Amount of Order	First Class	UPS		
			Order Total	
			UPS ❑ First Class ❑ *Shipping and handling must be added. See chart for charges.*	
$ 7.50 and under	1.00	4.00		
$ 7.51 to 12.50	1.50	4.25	**Subtotal**	
$12.51 to 25.00	3.50	4.50	**California Residents—Sales Tax** *Add 7.25% of subtotal.*	
$25.01 to 35.00	4.50	4.75		
$35.01 to 60.00	5.50	5.25	**Non-United States Residents** *Australia add 25%. All other locations: U.S. price plus 10% surface postage or 25% airmail.*	
$60.00 and over	6.50	5.75		
			Gift to Insight for Living *Tax-deductible in the United States.*	

Fed Ex and Fourth Class are also available. Please call for details.

If you are placing an order after January 1, 1997, please call for current prices.

Total Amount Due *Please do not send cash.*	$	

Prices are subject to change without notice.

Payment by: ❑ Check or money order payable to Insight for Living ❑ Credit card

(Circle one):   Visa   MasterCard   Discover Card   American Express   BankCard
(In Australia)

Number _____

Expiration Date _____   Signature _____

We cannot process your credit card purchase without your signature.

Name _____

Address _____

City _____   State _____

Zip Code _____   Country _____

Telephone (____) _____   Radio Station ____ ____ ____ ____

If questions arise concerning your order, we may need to contact you.

Mail this order form to the Processing Services Department at one of these addresses:

Insight for Living
Post Office Box 69000, Anaheim, CA 92817-0900

Insight for Living, Inc.
GPO Box 2823 EE, Melbourne, VIC 3001, Australia

Order Form
Canadian Residents
(Residents of the United States, Australia, and other international locations,
please use order form on reverse side.)

CTTCS represents the entire *Classic Truths for Triumphant Living* series in a special album
cover, while CTT 1–3 are the individual tapes included in the series. CTT represents this
study guide, should you desire to order additional copies.

CTT	Study guide	$ 6.50 ea.
CTTCS	Cassette series,	31.50
	includes all individual tapes, album cover,	
	and one complimentary study guide	
CTT 1–3	Individual cassettes,	7.48 ea.
	includes messages A and B	

Product Code	Product Description	Quantity	Unit Price	Total
			$	$

Amount of Order	Canada Post
Orders to $10.00	2.00
$10.01 to 30.00	3.50
$30.01 to 50.00	5.00
$50.01 to 99.99	7.00
$100 and over	Free

Subtotal	
Add 7% GST	
British Columbia Residents *Add 7% sales tax on individual tapes or cassette series.*	
Shipping *Shipping and handling must be added. See chart for charges.*	
Gift to Insight for Living Ministries *Tax-deductible in Canada.*	
Total Amount Due *Please do not send cash.*	$

Loomis is also available. Please
call for details.

*If you are placing an order after January 1,
1997, please call for current prices.*

Prices are subject to change without notice.

Payment by: ☐ Cheque or money order payable to Insight for Living Ministries
☐ Credit card

(Circle one): Visa   MasterCard   Number _____

Expiration Date _____   Signature _____
We cannot process your credit card purchase without your signature.

Name _____

Address _____

City _____   Province _____

Postal Code _____   Country _____

Telephone (___) _____   Radio Station ____ ____ ____ ____
If questions arise concerning your order, we may need to contact you.

Mail this order form to the Processing Services Department at the following address:

Insight for Living Ministries
Post Office Box 2510
Vancouver, BC, Canada V6B 3W7

Order Form
United States, Australia, and Other International Locations
(Canadian residents please use order form on reverse side.)

CTTCS represents the entire *Classic Truths for Triumphant Living* series in a special album cover, while CTT 1–3 are the individual tapes included in the series. CTT represents this study guide, should you desire to order additional copies.

CTT	Study guide	$ 4.95 ea.
CTTCS	Cassette series, includes all individual tapes, album cover, and one complimentary study guide	22.00
CTT 1–3	Individual cassettes, includes messages A and B	6.00 ea.

Product Code	Product Description	Quantity	Unit Price	Total
			$	$

Amount of Order	First Class	UPS
$ 7.50 and under	1.00	4.00
$ 7.51 to 12.50	1.50	4.25
$12.51 to 25.00	3.50	4.50
$25.01 to 35.00	4.50	4.75
$35.01 to 60.00	5.50	5.25
$60.00 and over	6.50	5.75

Order Total	
UPS ❏　First Class ❏ *Shipping and handling must be added. See chart for charges.*	
Subtotal	
California Residents—Sales Tax *Add 7.25% of subtotal.*	
Non-United States Residents *Australia add 25%. All other locations: U.S. price plus 10% surface postage or 25% airmail.*	
Gift to Insight for Living *Tax-deductible in the United States.*	
Total Amount Due *Please do not send cash.*	$

Fed Ex and Fourth Class are also available. Please call for details.

If you are placing an order after January 1, 1997, please call for current prices.

Prices are subject to change without notice.

Payment by: ❏ Check or money order payable to Insight for Living　❏ Credit card

(Circle one):　Visa　MasterCard　Discover Card　American Express　BankCard
(In Australia)

Number _____

Expiration Date _____　Signature _____
We cannot process your credit card purchase without your signature.

Name _____

Address _____

City _____　State _____

Zip Code _____　Country _____

Telephone (___) _____　Radio Station ____ ____ ____ ____
If questions arise concerning your order, we may need to contact you.

Mail this order form to the Processing Services Department at one of these addresses:

Insight for Living
Post Office Box 69000, Anaheim, CA 92817-0900

Insight for Living, Inc.
GPO Box 2823 EE, Melbourne, VIC 3001, Australia

Order Form
Canadian Residents
(Residents of the United States, Australia, and other international locations, please use order form on reverse side.)

CTTCS represents the entire *Classic Truths for Triumphant Living* series in a special album cover, while CTT 1–3 are the individual tapes included in the series. CTT represents this study guide, should you desire to order additional copies.

CTT	Study guide	$ 6.50 ea.
CTTCS	Cassette series,	31.50
	includes all individual tapes, album cover, and one complimentary study guide	
CTT 1–3	Individual cassettes, includes messages A and B	7.48 ea.

Product Code	Product Description	Quantity	Unit Price	Total
			$	$

Amount of Order	Canada Post
Orders to $10.00	2.00
$10.01 to 30.00	3.50
$30.01 to 50.00	5.00
$50.01 to 99.99	7.00
$100 and over	Free

Loomis is also available. Please call for details.

If you are placing an order after January 1, 1997, please call for current prices.

Prices are subject to change without notice.

Subtotal	
Add 7% GST	
British Columbia Residents *Add 7% sales tax on individual tapes or cassette series.*	
Shipping *Shipping and handling must be added. See chart for charges.*	
Gift to Insight for Living Ministries *Tax-deductible in Canada.*	
Total Amount Due *Please do not send cash.*	$

Payment by: ☐ Cheque or money order payable to Insight for Living Ministries
☐ Credit card

(Circle one): Visa   MasterCard   Number _____

Expiration Date _____   Signature _____
We cannot process your credit card purchase without your signature.

Name _____

Address _____

City _____   Province _____

Postal Code _____   Country _____

Telephone (___) _____   Radio Station ____ ____ ____ ____
If questions arise concerning your order, we may need to contact you.

Mail this order form to the Processing Services Department at the following address:

Insight for Living Ministries
Post Office Box 2510
Vancouver, BC, Canada V6B 3W7

cccc